W9-BSR-494

Heart Talks with Mother God

A Liturgical Press Book

THE LITURGICAL PRESS
Collegeville, Minnesota

Heart Talks with Mother God

Bridget Mary Meehan *and*
Regina Madonna Oliver

Illustrated by
Betsy Bowen, Barbara Knutson, and Susan Sawyer

To my niece and nephew Katie and Danny, whose love, creativity, and openness
led me to explore the nurturing love of Mother God,
and to all the children of the world.

Bridget Mary Meehan

To my grandniece, Laura Ann Forth;
my grandnephew, William Webster Oliver;
my goddaughter, Meghan Dotson;
and the many children whose lives have touched mine
in thirty years of teaching.

Regina Madonna Oliver

Illustrations:

Besty Bowen: *Mother Hen*, page 23; *Grandmother God*, page 25; *Mother Eagle*, page 27; and border, page 47.

Barbara Knutson: *God Birthing the World*, page 13; *The Parable of the Lost Coin*, page 15; *The Parable of the Leaven*, page 17; *Mary, Mother of Jesus, Shows Us God's Mothering Love*, page 29; title pages; and borders, pages 5 and 11.

Susan Sawyer: *God, a Nurturing Mother*, page 19; *Mother God Watches over You*, page 21; *Mary Shows Us the Givingness of God*, page 33; and borders, pages 7 and 45.

Cover Illustration: Barbara Knutson
Design/Art Direction: Ann Blattner

The Scripture quotations contained herein are from the New Revised Standard Version of the Bible, © 1989 by the Division of Christian Education of the National Council of the Churches of Christ in the United States of America, and are used by permission. All rights reserved.

1   2   3   4   5   6   7   8

Library of Congress Cataloging-in-Publication Data

Meehan, Bridget.
   Heart talks with Mother God / Bridget Mary Meehan and Regina
Madonna Oliver ; illustrated by Betsy Bowen, Barbara Knutson, Susan
Sawyer.
      p.   cm.
   ISBN 0-8146-2069-8
   1. Femininity of God. 2. Children—Prayer-books and devotions—
English. I. Oliver, Regina Madonna, 1931– . II. Title.
BT153.M6M44 1995
242'.62—dc20   95-6404
                                           CIP
                                           AC

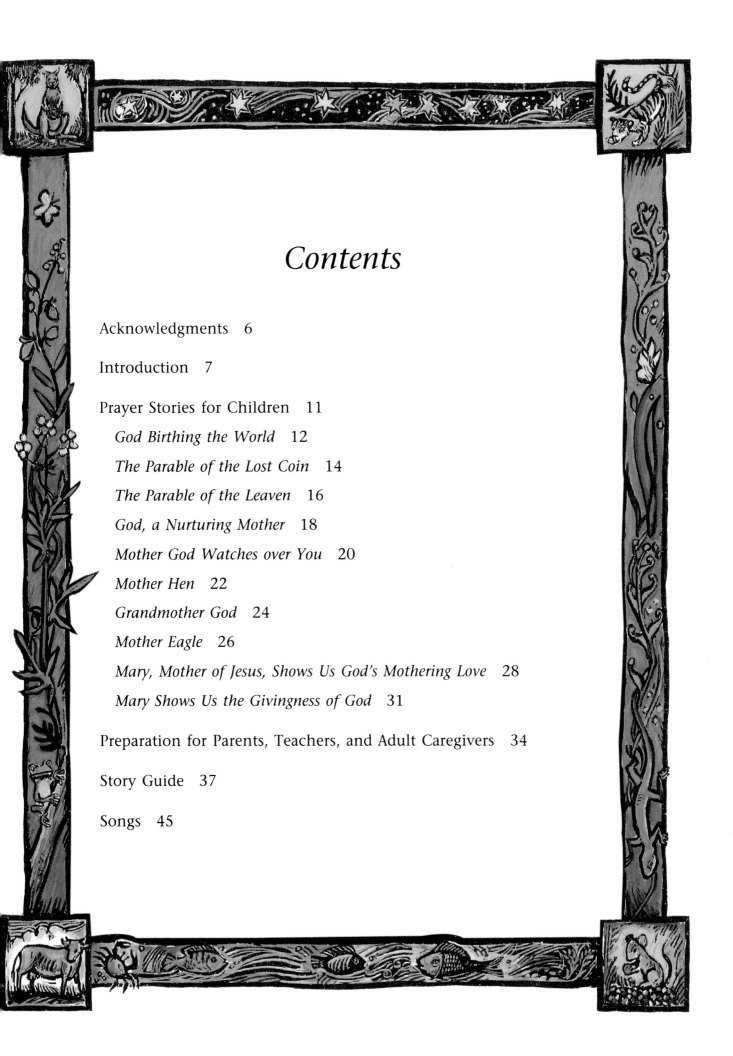

Contents

Acknowledgments

It is with deep gratitude that I thank my family and friends for their support in writing this book. I am grateful to my parents Jack and Bridie Meehan, my aunt Molly McCarthy, and my brothers and sisters-in-law Patrick and Valerie, Sean and Nancy, for their support and encouragement. I owe a debt of appreciation to Regina Madonna Oliver, Irene Marshall, Paul Wynants, John Weyand, Ray and Carol Buchanan, Debbie Dubuque, Ruth Reilly, Jeanette Kraska, Michal Morches, Maria Billick, Doris Mason, Kaye Brown, Peg and Bob Bowen, Sandy Volker, Daisy Sullivan, Francis Keefe, Joseph Mulqueen, Chaplain Joe Goudreau, Donna Mogan, and Anna Minassian. I thank, for their inspiration as the children in my life, my niece Katie, my nephew Danny, my goddaughter Megan Fitzgibbons and her brother Brendan, and my Irish cousins: Louise and Brendan, Darren, Eoin, Elaine, Clare, Brian, Shane, Darren, Ruth, James, Thomas, James, Brian, Niall, Sean, Colm, Orla, Avril, Elaine, Bill, Edna, Mathew, Dennis, John, Aidan, Noel, Lillian, Lorraine, and Esther.

I thank the children of Fort Myer community and their parents who have reflected the love of Mother God for me.

I am also grateful to Marcia Tibbitts, Betty Wade, Susan Curcio, Patricia Byrne, Patricia Muschamp, Kathleen Bulger, Marie Bonard, Eileen Dohn, George and Josephine Pida, members of St. Anthony's Gathering Church Group for their faith-sharing and support.

Bridget Mary Meehan

As I rejoice in a personal goal realized—to share in print with others some of my deepest insights—I reflect on those who have fed the intuitive and creative depths of my spirit where ideas gestate. I hesitate to begin a list for fear of forgetting even one of these gentle nurturers who "mothered" me.

Let me begin with my mother Ethel Marie Oliver, who read poetry to me daily from early toddler-stage; my father Harvey Oliver, who guided my musical appreciation to the classical and encouraged every step of instrumental learning; my brother David, who always affirms my gifts; and my nieces and nephews, who have been my "cheering squad": Jimmy and David Oliver, Barbara Forth, and Carol Tuohey.

I must list, as best I can, the other inspirers along the way: Sr. Rita McGarvey, I.H.M., Fr. Joseph McGarvey, Fr. John Weyand, Mother Claudia, I.H.M., Sr. Patricia Ann Carol, S.C.N., Fr. Stephen Usinowicz, O.C.S.O., Fr. Edward McCorkell, O.C.S.O., Rev. Tilden Edwards and the wonderful staff of Shalem Institute, Washington, D.C.; the teaching staff of the Washington Theological Union; Frances Lee Webster, my aunt, companion, and ego builder; and my dear friend Bridget Meehan, for her strong organizational gifts.

My gratitude I express for the loving support of Jack and Bridie Meehan, Virginia Limon, "Aunt" Molly McCarthy, Irene Marshall, Sally Ann Nelson, Phyllis Kessinger and Father David, Betty Fretz, Doris and Bob Schlesinger, Fr. Michael Travaglione, O.F.M., my pastor and colleague, the many friends from Fort Belvoir who constantly uphold and support, and my time-away friends on Chincoteague Island, Virginia: Fr. John Prinnelli, Catherine Nee, and the people of St. Andrew's Church.

Regina Madonna Oliver

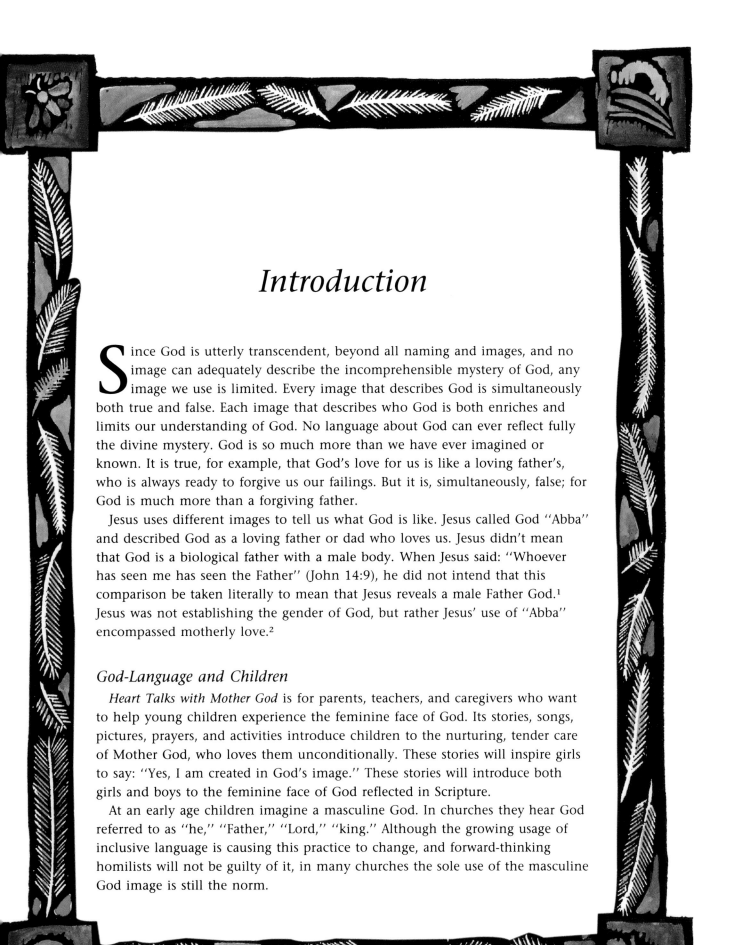

Introduction

S ince God is utterly transcendent, beyond all naming and images, and no image can adequately describe the incomprehensible mystery of God, any image we use is limited. Every image that describes God is simultaneously both true and false. Each image that describes who God is both enriches and limits our understanding of God. No language about God can ever reflect fully the divine mystery. God is so much more than we have ever imagined or known. It is true, for example, that God's love for us is like a loving father's, who is always ready to forgive us our failings. But it is, simultaneously, false; for God is much more than a forgiving father.

Jesus uses different images to tell us what God is like. Jesus called God "Abba" and described God as a loving father or dad who loves us. Jesus didn't mean that God is a biological father with a male body. When Jesus said: "Whoever has seen me has seen the Father" (John 14:9), he did not intend that this comparison be taken literally to mean that Jesus reveals a male Father God.[1] Jesus was not establishing the gender of God, but rather Jesus' use of "Abba" encompassed motherly love.[2]

God-Language and Children

Heart Talks with Mother God is for parents, teachers, and caregivers who want to help young children experience the feminine face of God. Its stories, songs, pictures, prayers, and activities introduce children to the nurturing, tender care of Mother God, who loves them unconditionally. These stories will inspire girls to say: "Yes, I am created in God's image." These stories will introduce both girls and boys to the feminine face of God reflected in Scripture.

At an early age children imagine a masculine God. In churches they hear God referred to as "he," "Father," "Lord," "king." Although the growing usage of inclusive language is causing this practice to change, and forward-thinking homilists will not be guilty of it, in many churches the sole use of the masculine God image is still the norm.

Masculine images of God are often understood literally by young children. They cannot comprehend a transcendent God who is beyond all images when what they hear and see present God in masculine metaphors only. Exclusive masculine images limit God and present a narrow and inadequate understanding of God. For example, Noreen, a young mother, in chatting about God with her four-year-old daughter Louise, referred to God as "she." Louise quickly disagreed with her mother: "No, Mommy, God is not a woman, he is a man." Her mother, taken by surprise, replied: "God can be female and male." But Louise went over to the bookcase and removed her children's prayerbook from the shelf and opened it up to a picture of God: "See, Mommy, God is a man who lives up on a cloud in the sky!"

Feminine Images of God in Scripture

Scripture uses feminine images to describe God's motherly womb love for us. For example: God is like a woman in labor who gasps, pants, and cries out as the contractions begin (Isa 42:14; Job 38:8; John 16:21). God is like a nurturing mother feeding her suckling infant at her breast (Isa 49:15; 66:11-13). "But I have calmed and quieted my soul, / like a weaned child with its mother; / my soul is like the weaned child that is with me" (Ps 131:2). God is like a midwife who guides the baby as it comes out of the mother's womb (Ps 22:9-10).

In the Song of Moses God describes herself in motherly imagery: "You were unmindful of the Rock that bore you; / you forgot the God who gave you birth" (Deut 32:18). God is like a mother eagle who teaches her young eaglets to fly (Deut 32:11-12). Like a strong mother who tries to protect her children from danger, God wants her children to know that she watches over them always (Eccl 4:11); God is like a grandmother who shares traditions and family secrets with her grandchildren (Ps 128:5); Mary, Mother of Jesus, shows us that God's mothering love always finds us and never lets us stay lost (Luke 2:42-48). Mary shows us that Mother God gives away her most precious gift, Jesus (Luke 2:1-16).

Jesus and Feminine God-Images

Jesus used feminine images to show us what God is like. Comparing the experience of a woman giving birth to the Christian's need for rebirth, Jesus revealed to Nicodemus the importance of being born of the Spirit in order to experience the kingdom of God (John 3:1-21). Jesus described God as a homemaker who searches for a lost coin (Luke 15:8-10) and as a bakerwoman who takes yeast and mixes it with flour to make bread (Matt 13:33; Luke 13:20). Jesus also tells us that God is like a mother hen who proudly gathers her chicks under her wings (Matt 23:37).

Rationale for the Use of Feminine Images

Teaching children to pray with feminine images of God at an early age is important because it provides a corrective to masculine-only images of God. Miriam Therese Winter, in a 1993 interview reported in *U.S. Catholic,* points out that "The biblical texts were written by men, assembled by men, edited by men, chronologically arranged by men, interpreted by men, preached upon by men, commented upon by men; therefore we have a very male perspective on the tradition."[3] Introducing children to the wealth of images for God, including both masculine and feminine metaphors, helps them to experience the richness of God's nature. It provides children with an inclusive way of exploring the divine mystery. It provides an antidote to centuries of predominately masculine imagery. It provides a more integrated and fuller understanding of who God is. Each feminine image of God presents another dimension or understanding of the mystery of God. It builds a theology of female and male created equally in God's image, free to develop their spiritual potential as partners and disciples. It gives little girls the same gender identification with God as little boys have always had. A girl's letter to God demonstrates this need: "Dear God, are boys better than girls? I know you are one but try to be fair."[4]

That girls and women can identify with God as daughters in the same way that boys and men unconsciously feel their connection to God as sons is the conclusion of Virginia Ann Froehle in *Called into Her Presence.*[5] When women embrace the Divine Feminine within them, they can experience a deeper sense of self-worth and empowerment. A woman shared, "Visualizing God as female makes me feel strong and confident. I am now more willing to be a risk-taker." Another woman commented that she discovered a deeper sense of connectedness with God and all creation, "When I pictured God as a woman in labor, panting and screaming through labor contractions, my image of creation changed. God was not far removed, up there somewhere, calling life forth; but, rather, was passionately involved in the birthing of creation. I had a deep sense that in God's womb all people, all God's creatures, all creation are somehow interconnected."[6]

Little boys and men equally need the balance which feminine imagery meditation provides, for their spiritual breadth has also been stunted by a predominance of masculine images. To cite Jann Aldredge Clanton's *In Whose Image:* "Men may not be aware of the extent to which masculine God-language also alienates men from portions of themselves, from others, and from God. . . . Patriarchal society has taught men not to reveal their weaknesses, especially to other men. Therefore when God is male, they cannot be completely open and honest even with God."[7]

When all images and concepts of God are masculine, men cannot experience as deeply as women God's Otherness. "There is a deep way in which it could be natural for men to see God through female images and women to seek God through male language, because . . . that could become a natural expression of Otherness." One middle-aged man shared the impact expanding his concept of God had on his spiritual life: "Praying with feminine images of God has been a powerful experience for me. I am discovering a new intimacy with God that I have never experienced before."[8]

God-Language and Spirituality

The inclusive God-language changes which the Church is preparing are as important for men as for women. Feminine images of God can expand men's spiritual potential by helping them discover and affirm the feminine in themselves. Men need no longer be afraid of their own healthy feminine attributes. "If our spirituality cannot embrace femininity, then it remains incomplete, unrealized. Spirituality in a man does not require a denial of the feminine. On the contrary, it is an affirmation of femininity as an essential part of ourselves—and of our God."[9] When the day dawns when we can comfortably call God "Mother" as well as "Father," both men and women will recognize themselves more fully as images of God.

Episcopal Bishop Moore contends that the Church must demonstrate a balance of gender for the spiritual growth of both men and women. He believes that the one reason that more women than men participate in Church is that our God-images are male. He reflects, "If the objects of devotion are only male, one cannot fully experience one's own spirituality. Everyone's prayer life is impoverished if we can only relate to a male God."[10]

Men and women need to be liberated from an understanding of religion that identifies God with maleness. We want to expand human consciousness of the divine to step beyond gender to gender-transcendence. God is always immensely more than any metaphor can provide. The God language and images we hand down to our children and grandchildren have the potential to transform everything—the way we see ourselves, the way we relate to God and to one another, our economic, political, social structures—indeed, to create a new paradigm where all human beings live in mutuality, justice, equality, and love.

Notes

1. Elizabeth Johnson, *She Who Is* (New York: Crossroad, 1992) 152.

2. Robert Hamerton-Kelly, *God the Father: Theology and Patriarchy in the Teaching of Jesus* (Philadelphia: Fortress, 1979) 65–81, 101.

3. Miriam Therese Winter, "Buried Treasures: Rediscovering Women's Roles in the Bible," *U.S. Catholic* 58 (June 1993) 11.

4. Eric Marshall and Stuart Hample, *Children's Letters to God* (New York: Simon and Schuster, 1966) n.p.

5. Virginia Ann Froehle, *Called into Her Presence* (Notre Dame, Ind.: Ave Maria Press, 1992) 35.

6. Bridget Mary Meehan, "Praying With Feminine Images of God, Part 2," *Religious Life Review* 32 (July/August 1993) 233.

7. Jann Aldredge Clanton, *In Whose Image* (New York: Crossroad, 1990) 93.

8. Sara Maitland, *A Map of the New Country: Women and Christianity* (London: Routledge and Kegan Paul, 1983) 189.

9. Mark Gerzon, *A Choice of Heroes: The Changing Faces of American Manhood* (Boston: Houghton Mifflin, 1982) 229.

10. Ibid., 222.

*Prayer Stories
for Children*

God Birthing the World

"In the beginning when God created the heavens and the earth . . . ."
(Genesis 1:1)

Meditation

In the beginning I had a wonderful new life inside me.
I grew bigger and bigger
  as the new life expanded and grew and took form.
It wanted to come out. It wanted to be.
All the marvelous things you see around you in the world:
  the moon and the sun
  the sparkling stars and shining rainbows,
  Mountains and lakes, rivers and oceans,
  Monkeys and kangaroos,
  Elephants and slithery snakes,
  Moths, beetles, and katydids,
  tigers and cows,
  dogs and cats, and your favorite animals,
roses and tulips, buttercups and daisies and your favorite flowers.
And you and you and you . . . .
All these splendid things were in the mind of your Mother God—
  growing, increasing, coming to full form,
And urging me to give birth to them:
And I said, "Let them be!"
And they were born!
I, God, gave birth to the moon, sun, and a million stars, rainbows, mountains
and lakes, rivers and oceans, monkeys and kangaroos, elephants, and snakes,
moths, beetles, katydids, tigers, cows, dogs and cats and your favorite animals,
and roses and tulips, buttercups and daisies and your favorite flowers.
All these I gave birth to because . . .
the best thing in your Mother God's mind was
you and you and you . . . .
And all the other things I made to give to you.

The Parable of the Lost Coin

"Or what woman having ten silver coins, if she loses one of them, does not light a lamp, sweep the house, and search carefully until she finds it? When she has found it, she calls together her friends and neighbors, saying, 'Rejoice with me, for I have found the coin I had lost.' Just so, I tell you, there is joy in the presence of the angels of God over one sinner who repents."   (Luke 15:8-10)

Meditation

(Mother God prepares to tell her story from the Bible.)

Did you ever lose your prettiest doll? your best ball? your favorite truck? your friendliest stuffed animal? Did you ask anyone to help you find your lost toy? Did you look for it by yourself? Where did you look for it? under the bed? behind the chair? in the garden? in the closet? How did you feel and act when you found it?

I want you to listen to a story Jesus tells us about your Mother God's love for you. My love for you is like a woman who had ten coins. She lost one and searched the whole house until she found it. One little coin, and she had nine others! But she looked and looked just for that one lost coin. And Jesus says *you* are very precious to Mother God, just like that little lost coin. If you are lost, God looks and looks for you, and never stops until you are found again!

"My dear, dear little one, don't be afraid if you feel lost. See me sweeping, bending down to see if my little lost coin is under the dining room table, or did it roll under the sink or behind the door? Watch me climb up on the chair to see if you are on top of the refrigerator. Now I am crawling on the floor, looking everywhere—even under the bed for you, my lost coin.

"Walk with me through every room of the house. We come to a small window in the baby's room. We look on the windowsill, and all of a sudden, there it is—in the flowerpot. Imagine that! How did you get in a flowerpot, my little lost coin? I run to you. I pick you up and hold you tight and we laugh and jump up and down for joy! Now I put the little lost coin safely with the other nine on a very special china dish. We are so happy that we plan the biggest party ever. You invite all your friends and rejoice with your Mother God, for she has found the lost coin."

The Parable of the Leaven

"The kingdom of heaven is like yeast that a woman took and mixed in with three measures of flour until all of it was leavened."

(Matthew 13:33)

Meditation

Did you ever help Mommy or Daddy bake bread? You began by getting a big bowl. Next you mixed a spoonful of yeast with some warm milk, and then you put lots of flour into the bowl. Then you took time off to let the mixture rise. The yeast sneaks into every part of the dough and makes it grow twice as big as when you began. Then you kneaded it, patted it, and placed it in a pan. You put it in an oven to bake. After a little while, you could smell the bread baking in your oven. Then when you took it out, the bread was golden brown, warm, light, and so delicious. You couldn't wait to share it with your family and friends.

I want you to listen to a story that Jesus tells us about your Mother God's love for you. Jesus said that the Kingdom of God is like the yeast that a woman took and mixed in with three measures of flour until it was leavened. This means that you are Mother God's yeast. Mother God takes your yeast of love, and like a bakerwoman, mixes you with others. With strong fingers she pats the people dough and shapes the loaf. Then she puts it into the oven to bake.

Mother God says, "You are my wonderful dab of yeast. I help you to be loving, kind, and helpful so that you can bring my love to everyone you meet. This love will move like the growing yeast into everyone around you. You will touch Mommy and Daddy, your brothers and sisters, your school friends. You will even touch with love the mail carrier who brings you letters and the gas station attendant who checks under the hood and fills your car with gas. When you are my yeast, you will spread my love far and wide. Then the whole world will become like one large, delicious, fresh-baked loaf of bread."

God, a Nurturing Mother

"... that you may nurse and be satisfied
   from her consoling breast;
that you may drink deeply with delight
   from her glorious bosom. . . .
and you shall nurse and be carried on her arm,
   and dandled on her knees.
As a mother comforts her child,
   so I will comfort you . . . ."
                              (Isaiah 66:11, 12b, 13a)

Meditation

Listen my child as your Mother God describes herself to you. . . .

"I am like a tender mother who cuddles, kisses, and holds you in her arms.

"I am like a caring mother who provides for your needs.

"I am like a comforting mother who dries your tears when you are sad.

"I am like a kind mother who always tells you how special you are.

"I am like a wise mother who teaches and guides you.

"I am like a happy mother who smiles, sings, plays, and dances with you.

"I am like a loving mother who tells you lots of times: 'I love you. . . . I believe in you. . . . Keep on trying. . . . I am proud of you. . . . I will always love you no matter what happens.'"

Did you ever meet someone who acted like your Mother God? Could you share your feelings about this person with Mother God?

Let Mother God hold you now. Let Mother God nurse you. Think of a time when you were hurt and tired and sobbing. Let Mother God into that time. Let her kiss away the tears. Let her soothing voice take away the pain. Rest in her arms.

Mother God Watches over You

Jesus tells us that with all the millions, even billions of birds in the sky, not even one sparrow will fall without God knowing it. Jesus tells you the same is true of you, because you are worth more than many sparrows.

(see Matthew 6:26)

Meditation

Mother God wants you to know that she loves you and watches over you each new day. When you wake up in the morning and see the sunshine, rain, or snowflakes, God, like a loving Mother, is watching over you.

"I watch over you when you are getting dressed; even when your socks don't match, or you forget to brush your teeth. I made you, and I like what I made, and I think you are beautiful.

"I watch over you as you eat your cereal and drink your juice. Even when you spill your juice or eat too quickly, I still smile at you. I watch over even when you lose your way. I send someone to show you the way.

"I watch over you even when you are sad or angry or afraid. I dry every tear and tell you again and again: 'I love you.'

"I watch over you even when your best friend runs away.

"I watch over you even when Mom and Dad don't see you slip and fall.

"I watch over you when your brother yells and your sister shouts: 'Go away.'

"I watch over you as you try so hard to read, write, and spell.

"I watch over you even when you are all alone at night in bed."

Before you go to sleep some night, look up to the heavens and see the stars twinkling brightly in the darkness above. They are one of the ways that your Mother God says: "I love you and I am always watching over you."

Mother Hen

"How often have I desired to gather your children together as a hen gathers her brood under her wings . . . ." (Matthew 23:37)

Meditation

Did you ever see a mother hen strutting across the barnyard with her tiny yellow chicks at her side? All the animals in the barnyard notice how proud mother hen is of her new babies. She spreads her strong wings over them as she scoots them up and down the barnyard on their tour of their new home.

Spotting Jersey, the cow, hard at work giving milk, the mother hen stops and says: "Jersey, I want you to meet my beautiful new baby chicks." "What beautiful chicks," Jersey moos, surveying the waddling, yellow fuzzballs.

"Neigh, neigh, good job, Mother Hen!" Roger, the horse, whinnies from the nearby stable door.

"Ruff, ruff, I'm happy to meet your new family too!" barks Muffin, the three-year-old cocker spaniel, as she dashes by Mrs. Hen's family.

"Meow, meow, I will not chase you today," teases Mickey, the large white cat, from her perch in the red maple tree.

In the Bible Jesus tells us that Mother God's love for us is like that of a mother hen's love. She loves to cuddle her chicks under her wings. This is the way Mother God is with you. Our Mother God is so proud of you and you and you that she tells everyone in heaven and on earth how beautiful you are!

Grandmother God

"The LORD bless you from Zion.
   May you see the prosperity of Jerusalem
   all the days of your life.
May you see your children's children.
   Peace be upon Israel!"

(Psalm 128:5-6)

Meditation

Did you ever bake cookies with your Grandmother? Did the kitchen feel cozy-warm and smell yummy? Did Grandmother let you lick the bowl clean? Did she pour tall glasses of cold milk for you to drink with her gigantic, delicious cookies? Did your Grandmother ever sew a beautiful outfit for you? Did your Grandmother ever take walks with you in the park and teach you how to feed the birds? Did your Grandmother ever tell you stories about long ago when she was your age? Did Grandmother show you pictures of your Mommy or Daddy when they were children? Did Grandmother ever share family secrets with you?

Did you know that Mother God is like a grandmother? Close your eyes now, and think about all the ways God loves you like a heavenly grandmother. Imagine Grandmother God inviting you to go for a walk to a beautiful place with her now. See her take you by the hand. Talk to Grandmother God from your heart. Tell her a special secret that you have wanted to share with someone for a long time. Notice that Grandmother God smiles as you whisper your secret in her ear. Now Grandmother God turns to you and gives you a big hug, saying: "I love you very much my child, I will always walk with you everyday of your life. Now I want to share a special secret with you." Listen carefully to Grandmother God as she whispers a special message in your ear.

Mother Eagle

"As an eagle stirs up its nest,
and hovers over its young;
as it spreads its wings, takes them up,
and bears them aloft on its pinions . . . ."
(Deuteronomy 32:11)

Meditation

Did you ever watch your Mommy or Daddy help your baby brother or sister to walk? When the baby stands up, they hold out their arms, call the baby to come to them, and clap with joy when baby takes a first step. If the baby falls down, Mommy or Daddy keeps encouraging the toddler to try again and again. They are always there, reaching out with love each time the baby falls. They never get tired of this game. They are giving their love to their beautiful little child.

God is like a mother eagle, the Bible tells us, who shows her eaglets how to fly. When mother eagle thinks her eaglets are ready, she swoops down and lets her little ones try their new wings. Squawking and fluttering, they go flying in the sky. If they get tired or afraid and squeal for help, mother eagle swoops below them and catches her frightened airborne babies with her strong, majestic wings. O what a scene to behold, eaglets proudly perched on mother eagle's wings soaring through bright, fluffy clouds on a sunny day.

Mother God wants you to try "your wings." She wants you to grow up and be a big girl, a big boy. You are to help others who need God's loving, motherly care. To do this, you will need to be brave and strong. There are things to be done that will be hard. They will take time and you will need to give away lots of love. You will need to do daring deeds—like cheering up people who are lonely and sad, visiting a sick neighbor, caring for the earth, and sharing with hungry and homeless people.

These are only a few of the many ways you can bring Mother God's love to the world. Perhaps you may think of more. Remember, if you are tired, or don't feel like giving love anymore, Mother God is beside you to show you how to be strong and daring like a mother eagle soaring through the sky with her baby eaglets on her wings.

Mary, Mother of Jesus, Shows Us God's Mothering Love

"And when [Jesus] was twelve years old, they went up as usual for the festival. When the festival was ended and they started to return, the boy Jesus stayed behind in Jerusalem, but his parents did not know it. Assuming that he was in the group of travelers, they went a day's journey. Then they started to look for him among their relatives and friends. When they did not find him, they returned to Jerusalem to search for him. After three days they found him in the temple . . . and his mother said to him, 'Child, why have you treated us like this? Look, your father and I have been searching for you in great anxiety.'"

(Luke 2:42-46, 48)

Meditation

God's book, the Bible, gives us lots of clues about what God is like, and how much God loves us like a Mother. In this story we see Mary, Jesus' beautiful Mother. Mary listened to God so perfectly when she was a little girl that she really shows us more than anyone else what our Mothering God is like.

In the story of Jesus and Mary that is called the Gospel According to St. Luke, Mary and Joseph have lost Jesus! Mary was sure Jesus was with his cousins in the big family group that travelled together. It was a long trip from Jerusalem to their home in Nazareth. At night they would stop for supper and camp out until morning. But when suppertime came, there was no Jesus. No one had seen him.

How worried Mary was! She and Joseph said goodbye to everyone, and hurried back all the way to the Holy City, Jerusalem. They looked up and down the streets and in any stores where they had stopped: "Have you seen Jesus?" they asked. "He is only twelve years old, and this is his first time away from our little village." They told the shopkeepers what he looked like and how he was dressed, but no one had seen him. Finally, after three days of searching, Mary and Joseph went back to the temple. As they entered they heard a boy's voice, asking questions; and the older voices of the Doctors of the Law answering. It was Jesus.

Mary was so excited. The worry wrinkles on Joseph's forehead gave way to smiling crinkles around his eyes. Mary ran to the side room where she heard the voices and burst through the door! "Child," she said, "why have you treated us like this? Look, your father and I have been searching for you in great anxiety."

Have you ever been lost from your Mother and Father? Did you ever get so excited about the toys in the toy store that when you looked around Mommy and Daddy were nowhere to be seen? Did Mommy and Daddy come looking for you? Where did they find you? Do you think Mommy or Daddy would ever stop looking for you if you were lost?

Our Mother God is like that—just like Mary, Jesus' Mother, God is always looking for us! The more lost we are, the more God looks and looks. And what is so wonderful is that God always, always finds us. Take time now to be with Mother God. Sit on her lap and let her tell you that she loves you the way Mary loves Jesus.

You can never, ever get lost from God, for she will always seek and find you. And you will be so glad to see God. You enjoy it so much when she holds you close and tells you you are beautiful. Say "thank you" to Mother God that you can never stay "lost." "Thank you" that she always knows where to find you, and that you are so special to her that she will never get tired looking for you. God will never, ever quit. Spend time in her arms, knowing you are safe.

Mary Shows Us the Givingness of God

"Joseph also went from the town of Nazareth in Galilee to Judea, to the city of David called Bethlehem, because he was descended from the house and family of David. He went to be registered with Mary . . . who was expecting a child. While they were there, the time came for her to deliver her child. And she gave birth to her firstborn son and wrapped him in bands of cloth, and laid him in a manger, because there was no place for them in the inn. In that region there were shepherds . . . ."

(Luke 2:4-8)

Meditation

Mary has a baby. Oh, how she loves him. She holds him and coos at him. She sings him a lullaby and rocks him. It is a very special moment. She feels very rich, like her baby is *all hers.*

But then there is a noise outside the stable. Someone calls out: "What do you want?"

"We want to see the newborn baby King. We were in the fields with our sheep when an angel of God told us to come to Bethlehem where we would find a newborn baby with his Mother. He is the promised one who will save us from sin."

Mary's lullaby stops. She holds her baby close to her heart and soothes him with the caress of her words: "It's all right, little one. It's all right."

The door of the stable opens and several shepherds and shepherd boys and girls step inside, along with a few stray sheep. One little shepherd is holding a soft, wooly lamb.

"We have come to see your baby, dear lady," the older shepherd tells her. "We want to do him honor. The angel says that he is the promised Savior!"

Mary smiles. But something inside her tugs. This is her baby! Now the shepherd is reminding her that Jesus is to belong to them too—and to everyone.

"May I hold him," asks the little shepherd, putting down the wooly lamb. "Oh, this lamb is a present for Jesus. She is my very own. I call her 'Rama,' but I want Jesus to have her."

Mary says, "I thank you, little shepherd. And Jesus thanks you, even though he is too little to say so."

Mary gives Baby Jesus to the little shepherd to hold and rock. She strokes Rama, running her fingers through her curly wool.

All the shepherds gather around the little shepherd. They coo at the new baby. They giggle when he screws his face up. They "ooooh" and "ahhh" when he opens his eyes. Each of them wants a turn to hold him.

Mary has given over her precious treasure. She knows Jesus is not hers only. Jesus is everyone's. Jesus is also *yours* to hold. Mary gives him to you too. Mary gives him to us! *Mary gives!*

God is like this. God gives. God gives her most precious gift—Jesus. God holds nothing back. Mary's giving reminds us that Mother God gives Jesus to you. Mother God gives Jesus to all of us! Mother God gives.

PREPARATION FOR PARENTS, TEACHERS, AND ADULT CAREGIVERS

Guiding Children into Mother-God Imaging

Heart Talks with Mother God is a resource for introducing young children to the depths of God's love for them revealed in the heart of Mother God. It provides parents, teachers, and other adult caregivers with a hands-on approach to "praying with" and reflecting on different images of God's motherly love found in the Bible. It presents powerful visual and verbal feminine images that introduce children to Mother God.

For children who have been abused by a father or other male, the traditional image of God as father often generates negative emotions. If we use the father image to teach them how to pray to God, they may feel God is abusive and may not be able to develop a personal relationship with God. Using the feminine image of God as mother can help these children experience the nurturing love of God. If, on the other hand, children have been abused by their mother or other women, the loving father image of God may bring healing.

The Mother God image can heal the difference between the love the children received and the love the children needed. Our loving God can reach deep into our past memories of unlove, neglect, or abuse and deeply heal us. In either case it is important to present loving images of God that children can relate to and that will minister to their spiritual needs.

Another consideration for the adult caregiver who is attempting to introduce a child to this form of meditation is the interpersonal relationship between this caregiver and the child in their day-to-day interaction. If the caregiver, now "prayer leader," is *the* authority figure in the child's life, this may affect his or her level of success in leading the child into contemplative prayer. Sometimes the mother may be the disciplinarian in the family. In other families it may be the father. This may impact on the parent's level of success as prayer leader. That, of course, depends on what "authority" means in

the relationship. Authoritarianism may prove to be detrimental, since in itself it is not a healthy form of authority practice. Each caregiver needs to analyze and consider his or her relationship with the child/children.

In the family setting one parent may have greater success in being the prayer leader than the other. It is better to be aware of one's talent in this respect and to take advantage of the gifts of the parent whose leadership in prayer is of greater profit in opening the child to the feminine experience of God.

One woman who reports on the result of her attempts to relate to a "Mother God" tells of a healing she experienced, which directly relates to the experience of growing up in a single-parent family in which the mother was the sole authority figure. Miriam told of experiencing a *block* in her ability to image a "mothering" God. She could not understand this, although scripturally the concept was sound, so she asked Mother God to show her what the problem was. Suddenly she heard her own voice, as a child, saying: "I don't want a *heavenly mother* telling me what to do!" With that came the realization that the experience of her mother as sole disciplinarian at the teenage time of her own struggle for autonomy had been a barrier to experiencing the "nurturing" aspect of God.

In the situation of the single-parent family, the mother-father role of the one parent may affect the effort to serve as prayer leader, just as it may affect any aspect of the parent-child interaction. This should not prevent the parent from the attempt to lead this form of contemplative experience! Its story and play-action components are naturally attractive to a child, and the parent-child togetherness in the experience has the potential to enhance their relationship in a loving way. There is also the possibility of a "healing of memories" such as the one related in the anecdote above.

If the father is the single parent and sole disciplinarian, it is just possible that a block to relating to a

"Fathering God" may exist, undetected, until prayer with a "father focus" is attempted. A father may be just as adept at guiding the child into a "Mother God" experience that is healing and life-giving as a female parent, and should not, therefore, abandon the effort of trying the technique with his child. Indeed, a "heart talk" with Mother God provides great richness for both father and child, offering a new and deep awareness of another aspect of the divine mystery, that of the feminine in God.

The guided meditations, illustrations, songs, and activities will help parents, teachers, and caregivers to instill in children the ability to think about, pray, imagine, and relate to God in feminine images as well as the traditional masculine images which are more familiar. *Heart Talks with Mother God* introduces children to a variety of Scripture images that describe the warm and caring tenderness of God's motherly love for us. The guided prayer meditations contained will help children experience the nurturing care of God who is our perfect Mother.

Play Prep

Each section of *Heart Talks with Mother God* begins with a *play prep* that can be used to prepare the children for the meditation. It involves creative, fun games, role playing, activities, etc., that help children actually experience Mother God's love. This *play prep* can be done a different day or time before the meditation and may be repeated after the meditation if the children seem to enjoy it. Parents, teachers, and other caregivers might choose to adapt these exercises to suit the needs of particular children.

Sacred Place

The next step is to create a *sacred place* for this meditation. Children love secret or special places to explore life. It is important to invite the child or children to find *their* special place each time they do one of these meditations. It could be under the table, behind a curtain, in a bed, on a rocking chair, in your arms, in a special prayer corner, etc. It is important that the children know that this is a "special place" where they will go for their *Heart Talks with Mother God.*

After the child or children arrive at their *sacred place,* invite the child/children to close their eyes and breathe slowly and deeply through the nose, in and out . . . in and out . . . for a minute or two.

Storytelling

With a calm, quiet, soothing voice read the *Heart Talk.* Pause between sentences or images so that children will have time to imagine. When you finish the meditation, allow quiet time for them to contemplate Mother God in a simple, wordless manner, as they rest in her arms. Being in the presence of Mother God is the attitude to foster during this quiet time.

Delighting in Mother God

One approach to try is to invite the child/children to rock for a while in Mother God's arms. The child/children do not do anything at this time. They delight in Mother God's love for them. The length of this quiet time will depend on the child's/children's age(s) and attention span. Then use one or more questions in the guide to help the child/children talk to Mother God about their feelings. Or, suggest that the children go to their "heart rooms," the place inside them where Mother God dwells. See preparations for parents, teachers, and adult caregivers in the appendix. Tell the child/children something like: "See Mother God in your heart room now. She loves you more than anyone in the whole world. Hear her call your name. See Mother God hug you."

Listening to Mother God

"Listen to Mother God as she talks to you. Mother God will not speak words that you can hear with your ears but with your heart." Then use one or more questions in the guide to help the child/children talk to Mother God about their feelings.

Saying Goodbye

When it is time to conclude the meditation, suggest something like: "Give Mother God one big hug, and whisper, 'I'll be back again,' as you slide from her lap. Now come back from your special quiet place to a 'sharing place' where we have our Bible enthroned. We will share with others anything you wish from your heart talk with Mother God."

Or say: "It's time to come from your heart room. Before you leave is there anything else you want to say or do with Mother God? Perhaps there is something that Mother God wants to say or do with you. Or perhaps you just want to say thank you and goodbye."

Sharing Time

"Open your eyes slowly and gently, take some deep, slow breaths. If you wish, yawn or stretch if this makes you feel good. When you are ready, you may wish to share with others something about Mother God, something you saw, heard, or felt when you sat on Mother God's lap, or when you were in your heart room with Mother God. Perhaps you have a question that you asked Mother God or something else that you would like to share with others about your heart talk."

The questions in the Story Guide for *Heart Talks with Mother God* may be helpful in getting the discussion underway. Sometimes, children at this age are so spontaneous that they will begin the discussion with little or no prompting. Each day the length, quality, and time spent in sharing may vary according to the child's/children's interest and age. However, it is important to spend a little time so they can share anything they wish to share and to invite them to ask questions. The child/children may come up with great games, activities, role-playing ideas that might deepen their relationship with Mother God. Be open to some amazing ideas, questions, and possibilities! Children have wonderful, beautiful imaginations. All adults have to do is provide children with a loving space to contemplate. As natural mystics and little prophets, our children will lead us to the heart of Mother God.

Songs

As an addenda to *Heart Talks with Mother God* are three songs. The optional use of a catchy melody with words that summarize the story may be used either as a conclusion or as an introduction to that experience, or can begin the sharing sessions.

The song "Mother God" is especially helpful as a kind of mantra to soothe children into the "delighting" or contemplative phase. To that purpose a lullaby melody was created.

The song "What Is Our God Like?" is more lively and may be a useful conclusion to each meditation time. Use just the stanza that fits the story at first. Since children love gesture, you may invent appropriate hand or body movements to accompany the words. Once the children have done several meditations, let them sing the old verses as well as the new one for today's prayer-story. Children love repetition; the singing of favorite songs over and over also drives home the prayer experience.

The song "I Clap My Hands," with its gestures for every verse, is especially appropriate for the meditation on Creation.

STORY GUIDE

God Birthing the World

PLAY PREP

To prepare for this meditation, a parent/teacher/care-giver might put out clay or play dough and invite the child/children to help make a whole array of things—all the things the child/children can think of to make. Make things with the child/children. Dialogue as you do it: "I think I'll make a _____." "Oh, look, I made _____."

Another activity that might be fun is to take a "Praise Walk." Invite the child/children to take a walk with you outdoors and name different gifts of creation that they see, hear, taste, or touch that they are happy God created. Participate in God's ongoing creation by planting a garden indoors or outdoors of children's favorite flowers or vegetables. Ask the child/children something like this: "Would you like to help God create?" "How can we do this?" "Maybe we could plant some seeds and watch them grow."

Another activity is to talk about how we help God create by keeping the earth clean and beautiful.

Have the Bible open on a table in a "Sharing Place" where you begin the Prayer Time.

Invite the child/children to find a special place to be for their "Heart Talk with Mother God" (under a table, behind a curtain, in a bed, on a rocking chair, in your arms, etc.).

Quiet the child/children by introducing each meditation with these or similar words:

Mother God wants to tell us a story from her wonderful book the Bible.

Imagine this loving mother inviting you to jump up on her lap. Why don't you jump up now. She will rock you and put her arms around you and hold you close to her heart. Listen to the steady beat of her heart. You are calm and peaceful as you feel how much Mother God loves you and how very special and very safe you are.

Listen closely as Mother God reads to you from her storybook, the Bible. She tells you how all things began.

LET MOTHER GOD TELL THE STORY

When you finish the meditation, allow quiet time for the child/children to contemplate Mother God in a simple, wordless manner.

One way to do this is to invite the child/children to close their eyes and rock awhile in Mother God's arms.

Then invite the child/children to talk to Mother God about their feelings, thoughts, insights, and ideas:

How does it feel to know that God made everything just for you?

How does it feel to know that God made you in her image?

What can you do to help Mother God care for creation?

What are your favorite plants, animals, people? Share with Mother God your special thanks for making them for you. Ask Mother God to help you take good care of the earth, flowers, plants, animals, family, friends. (Here it would be good to name specific flowers, plants, animals, family members, or friends that the child/children would recognize.)

Is there something you want Mother God to do for you? for your Mom? Dad? sisters? brothers? grandparents? aunts? uncles? cousins? friends? poor people? sad people? pets?

When it is time to conclude the meditation, you could suggest:

Give Mother God one big hug, and whisper: "I'll be back again," as you slide from her lap. Now come back from your special quiet place to a sharing place where the Bible is enthroned to share with others.

The Parable of the Lost Coin

PLAY PREP

To prepare for this Prayer Time, the parent/teacher/caregiver might role-play with the child/children. Actually "lose" a dime. Say to the child/children, "I had ten dimes and we were going out to spend them. We were going to buy _____. And now I've lost one. Can you help me find it?" And proceed to hunt everywhere.

Have the Bible open on a table in a "Sharing Place" where you begin the Prayer Time.

Invite the child/children to find a special place to be for their "Heart Talk with Mother God" (under a table, behind a curtain, in a bed, on a rocking chair, in your arms, etc.).

Quiet the child/children by introducing the meditation with these or similar words:

> Mother God wants to tell us a story from her wonderful book, the Bible.
>
> Imagine this loving Mother inviting you to jump up on her lap. Why don't you jump up now. She will rock you and put her arms around you and hold you close to her heart. Listen to the steady beat of her heart. You are calm and peaceful as you feel how much she loves you and how very special and very safe you are.
>
> Listen closely as Mother God reads to you from her storybook, the Bible. She tells you how much she loves you.

LET MOTHER GOD TELL THE STORY

When you finish the meditation, allow quiet time for the child/children to contemplate Mother God in a simple, wordless manner.

One way to do this is to invite the child/children to close their eyes and rock awhile in Mother God's arms.

Then invite the child/children to talk to Mother God about their feelings, thoughts, insights, and ideas:

> How does it feel to know that Mother God always looks for you and will find you even if you get lost?

How does it feel to know that Mother God will always love you no matter what happens?

Are there times when you feel lost or afraid?

What can you do to help someone who feels lost or afraid to be aware of Mother God's love?

When it is time to conclude the meditation, you could suggest:

> Give Mother God one big hug, and whisper: "I'll be back again," as you slide from her lap. Now come back from your special quiet place to a sharing place where your Bible is enthroned to share with others.

The Parable of the Leaven

PLAY PREP

To prepare for this Prayer Time, a parent/teacher/caregiver might involve the child/children in baking a small loaf of bread, explaining what yeast is and how it works.

Have the Bible open on a table in a "Sharing Place" where you begin the Prayer Time.

Invite the child/children to find a special place to be for their "Heart Talk with Mother God" (under a table, behind a curtain, in a bed, on a rocking chair, in your arms, etc.).

Quiet the child/children by introducing the meditation with these or similar words:

> Mother God wants to tell us a story from her wonderful book, the Bible.
>
> Imagine this loving Mother inviting you to jump up on her lap. Why don't you jump up now. She will rock you and put her arms around you and hold you close to her heart. Listen to the steady beat of her heart. You are calm and peaceful as you feel how much she loves you and how very special and very safe you are.
>
> Listen closely as Mother God reads to you from her storybook, the Bible. She tells you how much she loves you.

LET MOTHER GOD TELL THE STORY

When you finish the meditation, allow quiet time for the child/children to contemplate Mother God in a simple, wordless manner.

One way to do this is to invite the child/children to close their eyes and rock awhile in Mother God's arms.

Then invite the child/children to talk to Mother God about their feelings, thoughts, insights, and ideas:

> Do you like to help bake bread?
>
> Can you think of yourself as the yeast of love that touches everyone the way the yeast spreads to every part of the dough?
>
> How does it feel to know that Mother God is like a bakerwoman who kneads, shapes, and bakes bread?
>
> How can you spread your love like the yeast in the bread today?

When it is time to conclude the meditation, you could suggest:

> Give Mother God one big hug, and whisper: "I'll be back again," as you slide from her lap. Now come back from your special quiet place to a sharing place where your Bible is enthroned to share with others.

God, a Nurturing Mother

PLAY PREP

Take out a photo album and show the child some of his or her adorable baby pictures. Especially helpful are those of Mother holding or nursing the baby. Talk about these; about how cute the child was (and still is); about some of the personal things the child couldn't know unless the little stories are handed down. (My Mother used to tell my brother, over and over, how he would fall asleep every time he started to eat; she had to shake him, and even turn him upside down, to wake him up enough to finish nursing.) Family stories are fun to giggle together over.

If you are leading several children, have them bring baby pictures to share, and let them tell some of their little stories.

Have the Bible open on a table in a "Sharing Place" where you begin the Prayer Time.

Invite the child/children to find a special place to be for their "Heart Talk with Mother God" (under a table, behind a curtain, in a bed, on a rocking chair, in your arms, etc.).

Quiet the child/children by introducing the meditation with these or similar words:

> Mother God wants to tell us a story from her wonderful book, the Bible.
>
> Imagine this loving Mother inviting you to jump up on her lap. Why don't you jump up now. She will rock you and put her arms around you and hold you close to her heart. Listen to the steady beat of her heart. You are calm and peaceful as you feel how much she loves you and how very special and very safe you are.
>
> Listen closely as Mother God reads to you from her storybook, the Bible. She tells you how much she loves you.

LET MOTHER GOD TELL THE STORY

When you finish the meditation, allow quiet time for the child/children to contemplate Mother God in a simple, wordless manner.

One way to do this is to invite the child/children to close their eyes and rock awhile in Mother God's arms.

Then invite the child/children to talk to Mother God about their feelings, thoughts, insights, and ideas:

> Do you think that Mother God acts like anyone you know? Why?
>
> How would you describe Mother God? (nice? kind? loving? wise? etc.)
>
> When you imagine Mother God, what picture do you get in your mind? (young? old? big? small?) What is she wearing? What is she doing?
>
> If you could have a talk with Mother God now, what would you say?
>
> Do you have any questions you'd like to ask Mother God?
>
> Is there anything you want Mother God to do for you? for you Mom? Dad? sisters? brothers? grandparents? aunts? uncles? cousins? friends? lost children/people? pets?

When it is time to conclude the meditation, you could suggest:

> Give Mother God one big hug, and whisper: "I'll be back again," as you slide from her lap. Now come back from your special quiet place to a sharing place where we have our Bible enthroned to share with others.

Mother God Watches over You

Take some crayons and paper or finger paints and a piece of shiny white shelf paper, or some colored pencils and paper, and invite the child/children to draw a picture of a beautiful day—the way they see it from their window when they first get up. Suggest that they make it the kind of day that makes them glad they got up. Invite them to put themselves in the picture now, happy with the beautiful day Mother God has given them.

Have the Bible open on a table in a "Sharing Place" where you begin the Prayer Time.

Invite the child/children to find a special place to be for their "Heart Talk with Mother God" (under a table, behind a curtain, in a bed, on a rocking chair, in your arms, etc.).

Quiet the child/children by introducing the meditation with these or similar words:

> Mother God wants to tell us a story from her wonderful book, the Bible.
>
> Imagine this loving Mother inviting you to jump up on her lap. Why don't you jump up now. She will rock you and put her arms around you and hold you close to her heart. Listen to the steady beat of her heart. You are calm and peaceful as you feel how much she loves you and how very special and very safe you are.
>
> Listen closely as Mother God reads to you from her storybook, the Bible. She tells you how much she loves you.

LET MOTHER GOD TELL THE STORY

When you finish the meditation, allow quiet time for the child/children to contemplate Mother God in a simple, wordless manner.

One way to do this is to invite the child/children to close their eyes and rock awhile in Mother God's arms.

Then invite the child/children to talk to Mother God about their feelings, thoughts, insights, and ideas:

> How does it make you feel that Mother God is always watching over you every day?
>
> What does Mother God say or do for you as she watches over you?
>
> What would you like to say to your Mother God who watches over you?

> Is there anyone you want Mother God to watch over? your Mom? Dad? sisters? brothers? grandparents? aunts? uncles? cousins? friends? lost children/people? pets?

When it is time to conclude the meditation, you could suggest:

> Give Mother God one big hug, and whisper: "I'll be back again," as you slide from her lap. Now come back from your special quiet place to a sharing place where we have our Bible enthroned to share with others.

Mother Hen

PLAY PREP

The parent/teacher/caregiver should either (a) take the child/children to a farm setting where they can watch hens and chicks, ducks and ducklings, (b) visit a nearby nest very quietly where a mother bird, perhaps a robin, has her little ones under her wings, or where she is sitting on the eggs until they hatch, or (c) read the story "The Little Red Hen" from a picture book.

If the children are in a group, they could have fun playing "Little Red Hen and Chicks." They love it when Mother Hen says: "Who will help me eat the bread?" All the lazy animals who wouldn't help suddenly say: "I will." "No you shan't," says Little Red Hen. "You did not help me sow the seed; you did not help me reap the wheat . . . so you shall not eat the bread! Come my little yellow chicks, this bread is for you!"

Have the Bible open on a table in a "Sharing Place" where you begin the Prayer Time.

Invite the child/children to find a special place to be for their "Heart Talk with Mother God" (under a table, behind a curtain, in a bed, on a rocking chair, in your arms, etc.).

Quiet the child/children by introducing the meditation with these or similar words:

> Mother God wants to tell us a story from her wonderful book, the Bible.
>
> Imagine this loving Mother inviting you to jump up on her lap. Why don't you jump up now. She will rock you and put her arms around you and hold you close to her heart. Listen to the steady beat of her heart. You are calm and peaceful as you

feel how much she loves you and how very special and very safe you are.

Listen closely as Mother God reads to you from her storybook, the Bible. She tells you how much she loves you.

LET MOTHER GOD TELL THE STORY

When you finish the meditation, allow quiet time for the child/children to contemplate Mother God in a simple, wordless manner.

One way to do this is to invite the child/children to close their eyes and rock awhile in Mother God's arms.

Then invite the child/children to talk to Mother God about their feelings, thoughts, insights, and ideas:

Do you feel special? beautiful? strong? _____? now? Why? Imagine Mother God telling others about how beautiful, good, strong, and kind you are. How does that make you feel?

Who would you like Mother God to tell that you are beautiful? your Mom? Dad? sisters? brothers? grandparents? aunts? uncles? cousins? friends?

Do you have any special, beautiful family members or friends that you would like to talk with Mother God about?

When it is time to conclude the meditation, you could suggest:

Give Mother God one big hug, and whisper: "I'll be back again," as you slide from her lap. Now come back from your special quiet place to a sharing place where we have our Bible enthroned to share with others.

Grandmother God

PLAY PREP

Parents might take their child/children to visit Grandma or invite Grandma to your house for a special lunch. Share with Grandma that you want to help your child understand how God loves the way Grandma does. Or in a classroom setting have a "Grandmother's Day." Children may bring pictures of their Grandmas or something Grandma brought them, or they may invite Grandma to school. Talk about how Grandma shows she loves her grandchildren.

Have the Bible open on a table in a "Sharing Place" where you begin the Prayer Time.

Invite the child/children to find a special place to be for their "Heart Talk with Mother God" (under a table, behind a curtain, in a bed, on a rocking chair, in your arms, etc.).

Quiet the child/children by introducing the meditation with these or similar words:

Mother God wants to tell us a story from her wonderful book, the Bible.

Imagine this loving Mother inviting you to jump up on her lap. Why don't you jump up now. She will rock you and put her arms around you and hold you close to her heart. Listen to the steady beat of her heart. You are calm and peaceful as you feel how much she loves you and how very special and very safe you are.

Listen closely as Mother God reads to you from her storybook, the Bible. She tells you how much she loves you.

LET MOTHER GOD TELL THE STORY

When you finish the meditation, allow quiet time for the child/children to contemplate Mother God in a simple, wordless manner.

One way to do this is to invite the child/children to close their eyes and rock awhile in Mother God's arms.

Then invite the child/children to talk to Mother God about their feelings, thoughts, insights, and ideas:

What do you like about Grandmothers?

What are some ways that your Grandmother reminds you of Grandmother God?

Have you ever shared a secret with Grandmother God?

What secret did you share with Grandmother God?

What secret did Grandmother God share with you?

How did you feel about this secret?

Are there any questions that you would like to ask Grandmother God?

When it is time to conclude the meditation, you could suggest:

Give Mother God one big hug, and whisper: "I'll be back again," as you slide from her lap. Now come back from your special quiet place to a sharing place where we have our Bible enthroned to share with others.

Mother Eagle

PLAY PREP

Parents, if you have a video of your child/children learning to move from crawling to walking, show it. Enjoy it with them. You might freeze frame a shot. Then suggest that each pretends he or she is a "Mommy" or "Daddy" teaching a baby brother or sister to walk. Another activity that might be fun is to invite the child/children to play "mother eagle." Put on some "soaring music" and let them stretch their wings and "fly" around the house or yard with their baby eaglets on their wings.

Some other variations on the same idea are to suggest that the child/children teach their dolls or stuffed animals "to walk" or "to fly" or to recommend that the child/children pretend that they are baby eagles learning how to fly. The adult could also join in the "pretend play"!

Have the Bible open on a table in a "Sharing Place" where you begin the Prayer Time.

Invite the child/children to find a special place to be for their "Heart Talk with Mother God" (under a table, behind a curtain, in a bed, on a rocking chair, in your arms, etc.).

Quiet the child/children by introducing the meditation with these or similar words:

> Mother God wants to tell us a story from her wonderful book, the Bible.
>
> Imagine this loving Mother inviting you to jump up on her lap. Why don't you jump up now. She will rock you and put her arms around you and hold you close to her heart. Listen to the steady beat of her heart. You are calm and peaceful as you feel how much she loves you and how very special and very safe you are.
>
> Listen closely as Mother God reads to you from her storybook, the Bible. She tells you how much she loves you.

LET MOTHER GOD TELL THE STORY

When you finish the meditation, allow quiet time for the child/children to contemplate Mother God in a simple, wordless manner.

One way to do this is to invite the child/children to close their eyes and rock awhile in Mother God's arms.

Lead the child/children to do the following imaginary exercise:

> Imagine you are an eaglet learning to fly. Mother eagle takes you out of the nest, places you on her majestic wings for your first flight. Off into the blue sky, mother eagle takes you on an exciting ride. Then all of a sudden, mother eagle tells you it's time for you to try your new wings. A little nervous at first, but very excited, you start to fly. Up and down through the clouds, you fly, the wind pushing you faster and faster. You look down below and who do you see? Why, it's mother eagle right there, looking mighty proud of you, her little eaglet!

Invite the child/children to discuss their feelings, ideas, insights, and experiences with any of the following questions:

> How does it feel to fly high up in the sky? Were you afraid? Does mother eagle pick you up on her wings if you get tired or afraid? Are you looking forward to flying by yourself soon again?
>
> Did you ever do something to help someone who was lonely or sad, poor or homeless? How can you give love today to someone who needs a smile or a helping hand?
>
> Did you ever do a kind deed for someone who was mean to you?
>
> What can you do to take better care of your pets? plants? flowers? the earth?
>
> Are there ways you can help your family take better care of your home? Give the child/children a few suggestions, such as picking up clothes and toys, wiping up spills, turning off lights and water faucets when finished, recycling plastics and newspapers.
>
> Ask Mother God to help you love others even when it is hard to do so.

When it is time to conclude the meditation, you could suggest:

> Give Mother God one big hug, and whisper: "I'll be back again," as you slide from her lap. Now come back from your special quiet place to a sharing place where we have our Bible enthroned to share with others.

Mary, Mother of Jesus, Shows Us God's Mothering Love

PLAY PREP

Suggest that the child/children play hide and seek. Say something like: "When you play hide and seek it is no fun if the person who is 'It' can't find you, is it?" Invite the child/children to take turns at this game so they can "feel" how wonderful it feels to be found. Another activity would be to have the child/children dramatize or role-play this Scripture scene.

Have the Bible open on a table in a "Sharing Place" where you begin the Prayer Time.

Invite the child/children to find a special place to be for their "Heart Talk with Mother God" (under a table, behind a curtain, in a bed, on a rocking chair, in your arms, etc.).

Quiet the child/children by introducing the meditation with these or similar words:

> Mother God wants to tell us a story from her wonderful book, the Bible.
>
> Imagine this loving Mother inviting you to jump up on her lap. Why don't you jump up now. She will rock you and put her arms around you and hold you close to her heart. Listen to the steady beat of her heart. You are calm and peaceful as you feel how much she loves you and how very special and very safe you are.
>
> Listen closely as Mother God reads to you from her storybook, the Bible. She tells you how much she loves you.

LET MOTHER GOD TELL THE STORY

When you finish the meditation, allow quiet time for the child/children to contemplate Mother God in a simple, wordless manner.

One way to do this is to invite the child/children to close their eyes and rock awhile in Mother God's arms.

Then invite the child/children to talk to Mother God about their feelings, thoughts, insights, and ideas:

> Have you ever been lost? If so, did you feel scared or afraid?
>
> What did your parents say and do when you were lost?
>
> What did your parents say and do when you were found?

> Did you ever hide from your mother behind curtains, under a table? anywhere else? Do you remember what your mother said and did when she found you?
>
> If you were to play hide and seek with Mother God, where would you go to hide? Do you think Mother God would find you? Why?

When it is time to conclude the meditation, you could suggest:

> Give Mother God one big hug, and whisper: "I'll be back again," as you slide from her lap. Now come back from your special quiet place to a sharing place where we have our Bible enthroned to share with others.

Mary Shows Us the Givingness of God

PLAY PREP

Get out of a Christmas storage box the figurines from a Christmas manger scene (or, if the creche is an expensive one, buy some inexpensive pieces depicting Mary, Joseph, Baby Jesus, Angel, shepherd, and sheep). Invite the child/children to hold the figurines. Who is this? Invite the child/children to play with these figurines. Ask the child/children to dramatize the Christmas story with them. If the child/children don't recognize them (this could be the case with a three- or four-year-old who has not used the figurines in a familiar way, or who has not heard the Nativity story each year), you may need to tell the foundational story of the birth of Jesus.

THE GIVING GAME

Wrap some presents. Then at meditation time say something like:

> We are going to play the giving game. I have all these presents to give to you. Will you give one away? Will you give more than one? Whom will you give it to?

Parents could adapt a family tradition of giving away homemade presents which the children have helped to make to the needy several times a year. Another custom is to ask each child to give away a favorite toy to a needy child at Christmas each year.

Parents could also read or tell the child/children the Christmas story as given in the Luke 2:1-20. Invite the child/children to dramatize a radio or TV movie special of the Christmas story or of the meditation found on pages 31–32.

Invite the child/children to pretend that they are "Mother God." Tell the child/children you would like to interview them about how it feels to be "Mother God," the perfect mother who gives and shares with others. Some possible questions to ask are:

> Mother God, do you ever get tired of giving and giving to everyone in the whole world?
>
> Mother God, could you tell me some things I could share with others?
>
> Mother God, why do you love me so much?

Then suggest that you switch roles. Parents/teachers/adult caregivers then pretend that they are "Mother God." Invite the child/children to interview you asking any questions that come to mind. Fabricate a pretend microphone, and enjoy their probing queries!

Have the Bible open on a table in a "Sharing Place" where you begin the Prayer Time.

Invite the child/children to find a special place to be for their "Heart Talk with Mother God" (under a table, behind a curtain, in a bed, on a rocking chair, in your arms, etc.).

Quiet the child/children by introducing the meditation with these or similar words:

> Mother God wants to tell us a story from her wonderful book, the Bible. Do you remember how God's book, the Bible, reminds us how much our God is like a perfect mother? Have you ever met a "perfect mother?" Is your mother a "perfect mother"? It is hard to find a real life human person who is completely perfect, isn't it? That is why it helps us to think about the stories the Bible tells about Jesus' Mother, Mary.
>
> We know that Jesus is God's Son and is truly God and truly human, all in one. We know that Mary, his lovely mother, said yes to God's plan, that God's precious Child should become human, become a baby within her womb, and be born just like you and I were born. Jesus would grow up just

the way we do, and learn, and finally teach us by showing us just what God is like!

In this story from the Bible we can look at Mary, Jesus' mother. She is the perfect mother of the perfect baby. We can say: "Look at this picture of Mary at the time her baby is born—and you will see with your own eyes what God is like. Imagine this loving Mother inviting you to jump up on her lap.

> Why don't you jump up now. She will rock you and put her arms around you and hold you close to her heart. Listen to the steady beat of her heart. You are calm and peaceful as you feel how much she loves you and how very special and very safe you are.
>
> Listen closely as she reads to you from her storybook, the Bible. She tells you how much she loves you.

LET MOTHER GOD TELL THE STORY

When you finish the meditation, allow quiet time for the child/children to contemplate Mother God in a simple, wordless manner.

One way to do this is to invite the child/children to close their eyes and rock awhile in Mother God's arms.

Then invite the child/children to talk to Mother God about their feelings, thoughts, insights, and ideas:

> When Mary lets you hold the baby Jesus, what do you say to Mary? to Mother God?
>
> Can you name things Mother God has given to you? What do you say to her about this?
>
> Are you willing to share your things with others the way God shares with you? Talk to Mother God about this.
>
> How will you try today to share a toy, game, a treat, with someone else? Ask Mother God to help you be more giving each day.

When it is time to conclude the meditation, you could suggest:

> Give Mother God one big hug, and whisper: "I'll be back again," as you slide from her lap. Now come back from your special quiet place to a sharing place where we have our Bible enthroned to share with others.

Mother God, Mother God

(A song for settling into meditation)

Mo-ther God, Mo-ther God   on your lap   hold   me!

I'm   not a-fraid   when   your   arms en-fold   me.

Mo-ther God, Mo-ther God,   how   I   love you!

Sing "What Is Our God Like" for each meditation in *Heart Talks with Mother God.*

MEDITATION 1—*God Birthing the World*

Will you tell me, will you tell me,
What is our God like?
God is like a pregnant mother birthing her child.
Earth and sky and oceans, she thought of them and
    made them;
Living things created—God gave it all to us!

MEDITATION 2—*The Parable of the Lost Coin*

Will you tell me, will you tell me,
What is our God like?
God is like a woman
Searching for her lost coin.
All around the household
She looks in every corner;
Then, at last, she finds it
And celebrates for joy!

MEDITATION 3—*The Parable of the Leaven*

Will you tell me, will you tell me,
What is our God like?
God is like a woman baking,
Kneading the dough.
Right into her mixture
She puts a little yeast cake,
Spreads throughout the dough, and
the yeast will make it rise.

MEDITATION 4—*God, a Nurturing Mother*

Will you tell me, will you tell me,
What is our God like?
God is like a tender Mother
cuddling her child.
When you cry, she comforts;
She dries away your crying;
Tells you how she loves you
And always, always will.

MEDITATION 5—*Mother God Watches over You*

Will you tell me, will you tell me,
What is our God like?
God is like a caring mother
Bringing up her child.
When you wake each morning, God is watching o'er you;
All day long she's with you;
She watches while you sleep.

MEDITATION 6—*Mother Hen*

Will you tell me, will you tell me,
What is our God like?
Like a Mother Hen protecting
all her little chicks.
Proudly she shows them;
Fondly she feeds them;
Then beneath her wings she will
keep them safe and warm.

MEDITATION 7—*Grandmother God*

Will you tell me, will you tell me,
What is our God like?
God is like a dear grandmother
With her sweet grandchild.
How she loves to be with you;
How she loves to watch you;
How she loves to play with you
Giving you a hug.

MEDITATION 8—*Mother Eagle*

Will you tell me, will you tell me,
What is our God like?
I will tell you God is like a caring mother bird.
Like a mother eagle she carries on her wings
All her little eaglets
teaching them to fly.

MEDITATION 9—
Mary, Jesus' Mother, Shows Us God's Mothering Love

Will you tell me, will you tell me,
What is our God like?
God is like our mother Mary looking for her child.
For three days she searched for him
Praying she would find him.
Then within the temple she heard his gentle voice.

MEDITATION 10—*Mary Shows Us the Givingness of God*

Will you tell me, will you tell me,
What is our God like?
God is like the Blessed Mother
holding up her child.
"Here is Baby Jesus;
Would you like to hold him?"
All she has, she offers.
And God loves this way, too.

What Is Our God Like

I Clap My Hands

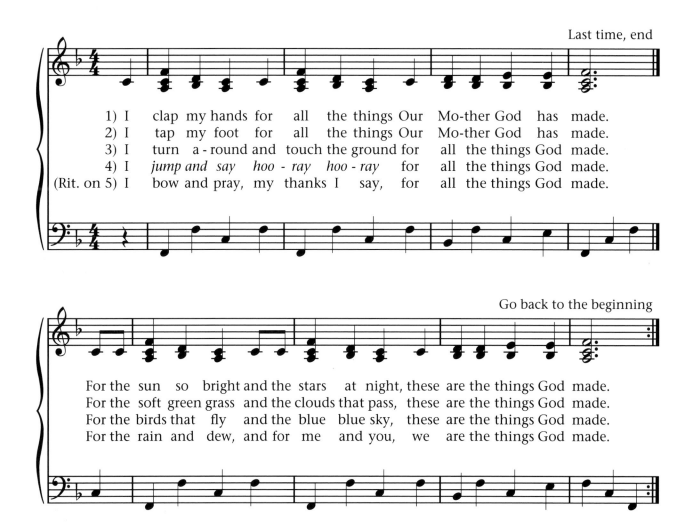

Last time, end

1) I clap my hands for all the things Our Mo-ther God has made.
2) I tap my foot for all the things Our Mo-ther God has made.
3) I turn a-round and touch the ground for all the things God made.
4) I *jump and say hoo-ray hoo-ray* for all the things God made.
(Rit. on 5) I bow and pray, my thanks I say, for all the things God made.

Go back to the beginning

For the sun so bright and the stars at night, these are the things God made.
For the soft green grass and the clouds that pass, these are the things God made.
For the birds that fly and the blue blue sky, these are the things God made.
For the rain and dew, and for me and you, we are the things God made.

This is an action song.

STANZA 1

The child/children can be given a gesture for: "The sun so bright" *(make a circle with the fingers of both hands up in the air above the head);* "and the stars of night" *(point to three stars on "stars of night").*

STANZA 2

The child/children clap or tap their toes, etc., when singing "Our Mother has made" and "these are the things God made."

STANZA 3

On the words "turn a-round" the child/children turn. On "touch the ground" they bend and touch the floor.

STANZA 4

On the verse "jump and say," the child/children jump in place.

"Hooray! Hooray!" can be shouted instead of sung.

STANZA 5

"I bow and pray, my thanks I say" *should ritard.* The child/children bow their heads and fold their hands.